THE STORY OF EASTER

Text by Mary Joslin
Illustrations copyright © 1998 Jackie Morris
This edition copyright © 2005 Lion Hudson

The moral rights of the author and illustrator
have been asserted

A Lion Children's book
an imprint of
Lion Hudson plc
Mayfield House, 256 Banbury Road,
Oxford OX2 7DH, England
www.lionhudson.com
ISBN 0 7459 4937 1

First edition 2005
1 3 5 7 9 10 8 6 4 2 0

A catalogue record for this book is available
from the British Library

Typeset in 15/20 BerkeleyOldstyle Book BT
Printed and bound in Singapore

THE STORY OF EASTER

MARY JOSLIN ✲ JACKIE MORRIS

LION
CHILDREN'S

THE STORY OF EASTER is about God and people and the friendship between them.

It begins in the very beginning, when God made heaven and earth.

At that time, God created a paradise garden for the first man and the first woman. They were God's friends and knew nothing about bad things. Everything was very, very good.

Then, one day, they chose to know about bad things. The world became a cruel place. Their friendship with God was broken.

Hundreds and thousands of years went by. People on earth longed to be close to God again, and God wanted to bless them.

One day, God sent the
Angel Gabriel to a town
called Nazareth. The angel
had a message for a young
woman named Mary.

'Peace be with you,' said
the angel. 'God has chosen
you to bear a son. You will
name him Jesus. He will be
called the Son of God.'

As the angel talked, Mary
began to understand. 'I will
do as God wants,' she
agreed.

About that time, an order came from the emperor in Rome. Everyone had to go to their home town and register to pay him taxes.

Mary travelled to Bethlehem with her husband-to-be, Joseph. The town was crowded with travellers, so the couple had to shelter in a stable.

There, Mary's baby was born.

On the hills nearby, shepherds were watching over their sheep. Suddenly, an angel appeared in the night sky, shining with all the brightness of heaven.

'Do not be afraid,' said the angel. 'I bring good news. A child has been born in Bethlehem: the one God has chosen to rescue all the world.

'You will find him wrapped in swaddling clothes and lying in a manger.'

All at once the sky was filled with angels singing praise to God. Then they vanished back into heaven.

'Let's go to Bethlehem,' said the shepherds. 'We must find out if any of this is true.'

They found Mary and Joseph and the baby, just as the angels had said.

Jesus grew up to be a good and obedient son. The people of Nazareth, where he lived, knew him simply as the local carpenter.

Then, when Jesus was about thirty, he became a preacher and a healer.

Crowds gathered to listen to him.

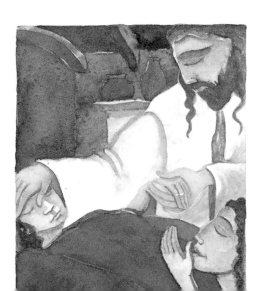

'Is anyone here poor or unhappy or downtrodden?' he asked. 'Does anyone think they're not good enough to please God? Here is good news: God will bless you. You can be part of God's kingdom.

'Is there anyone here who is rich or important? Anyone who thinks they already have the good things in life? Beware! If you forget to live as God wants, in the end you will be left with nothing.'

Jesus' preaching was not popular in Nazareth. Soon, he had to make his home in nearby Capernaum, on the shore of Lake Galilee.

He preached to the crowds there, and made friends with some of the local fishermen.

One day, he borrowed a boat as a place from which to preach. When he had finished, he spoke to the owner, Simon: 'Push your boat further out and let the nets down.'

'It will be a waste of time,' replied Simon. 'We fished all night and caught nothing.'

Even so, he did what Jesus asked. At once the nets were so full of fish that Simon and his friends struggled to land them.

'Don't be so amazed,' said Jesus. 'It's a sign. Leave your job of catching fish. Follow me, and help me gather people instead.'

The men came at once.

One day, some mothers
came with their children.
'We want Jesus to bless
them,' they explained to
Jesus' friends.
    'Our Master is too busy!'
came the reply.

'I am not too busy,' said
Jesus. 'Let the children come
to me. Don't try to stop
them. They are welcome
in God's kingdom.'

Indeed, Jesus welcomed all kinds of people: children and old people, women and men, rich and poor, strong and weak.

He healed many who were sick.

He taught all his listeners how to live as God's friends: 'Love God above all. Be faithful and obedient.

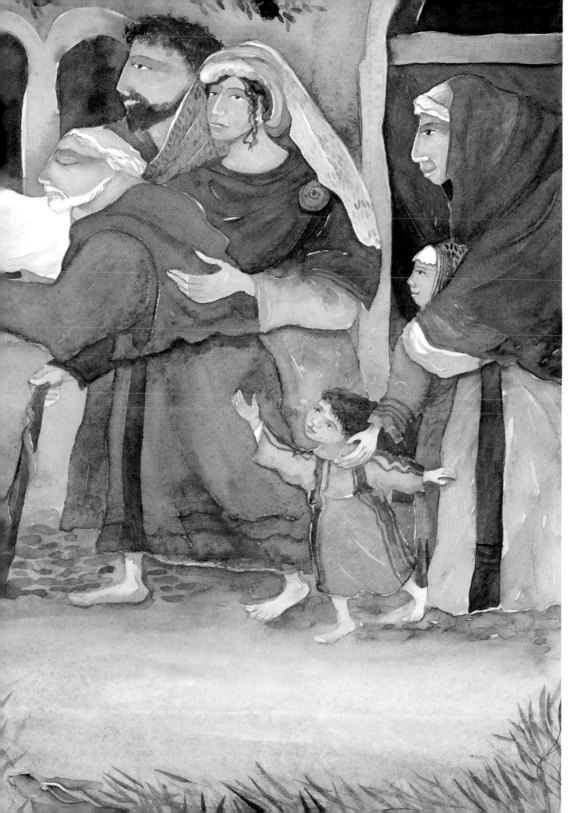

'Love one another.

'Do good to everyone, even those who hate you. Pray for the people who treat you badly.

'Forgive one another, and God will forgive you.'

Many people believed what he said and became his devoted followers.

All the while, the religious
leaders were growing uneasy.
  'Who is this Jesus whom
people follow?' they asked.
'We are not sure that his
teaching is correct.
  'We are not sure that he
respects God's laws – the
laws we try so hard to teach
people.'

'I saw him break the law about the Sabbath,' said one. 'It's meant to be a day of rest, but he healed a man right in the middle of the Sabbath meeting.'

'That's wicked,' they all agreed. They did not want to believe that his power to heal came from God. Instead, they plotted to get rid of him.

Their chance came when Jesus was in Jerusalem for the great festival called Passover. One of Jesus' friends told the religious leaders where they could find him all alone.

Jesus was praying in an olive grove named Gethsemane when soldiers arrived to arrest him.

The religious leaders accused him of being disrespectful to God; but that was not enough to condemn him.

They took him to the Roman governor in Jerusalem, Pontius Pilate. 'This man is a rebel,' they claimed. 'The people treat him like a king. He deserves to be executed.'

Pilate was not convinced, but crowds outside his palace were noisy and angry. 'Crucify him! Crucify him!' they shouted.

Pilate handed Jesus over to the soldiers. On a hill outside the city, they nailed him to a cross.

Two other men were crucified at the same time. One of them joined the angry crowds in jeering at Jesus.

'Aren't you God's chosen one then,' he said. 'Jesus Christ, our Messiah? Save yourself if you are. And save us too!'

'Leave him alone,' cried the other man. 'He's done nothing wrong. We're criminals and we know it.' Then he spoke to Jesus: 'Remember me when you come as king.'

'I promise,' said Jesus, 'that you will be in paradise with me today.'

Round about noon, the sun stopped shining and the sky went as dark as night. Jesus called out to God: 'Father, in your hands I place my spirit.' Then he died.

A wealthy man named Joseph went and asked Pilate for Jesus' body. He and his helpers wrapped it in a linen sheet. They carried it to a tomb cut into solid rock and placed it inside. The sun was setting: the Sabbath day of rest was about to begin.

Hurriedly, they rolled the stone door shut and went away.

The day after the Sabbath was Sunday. Early in the morning, some women who had been followers of Jesus went to the tomb. They wanted to prepare the body properly for burial.

To their amazement, the stone door had been rolled aside. Jesus' body had gone. As they stood there wondering what to do, two people in bright shining clothes appeared.

'Why are you looking among the dead for someone who is alive?' asked the angels. 'He is not here. He has risen to life.'

Over the next few days, Jesus appeared many times to his followers. He explained everything to them.

From the beginning, people had chosen the wrong path, and it had led to suffering. Jesus had come from God to the very heart of human suffering and died in agony. By rising again, he had shown the world the power of God's love: the love that welcomes people into heaven – as God's friends once again.

Other titles from Lion Children's Books

Easter: The Everlasting Story   Lois Rock & Christina Balit

The Story of the Cross   Mary Joslin & Gail Newey

First Festivals: Easter   Lois Rock